To Dear Christopher
with love from
Nanna Palmer
XX

Soccer Secrets of the Stars

IAN HUTCHINSON AND
PAUL TREVILLION

Soccer Secrets of the Stars

PELHAM BOOKS

First published in Great Britain by
PELHAM BOOKS LTD
52 Bedford Square
London, WC1B 3EF
1973

ISBN 0 7207 0533 9

Phototypeset by Filmtype Services Limited, Scarborough, in eleven on fourteen point. Printed in Great Britain by Hollen Street Press Ltd., at Slough on paper supplied by P. F. Bingham Ltd., and bound by Dorstel Press, Harlow

Contents

Ian Hutchinson Looks at the Stars

How does a star footballer rate the stars he plays with or against every week? How does he rate their ability? Why is one better than another? How do experts assess talent at this level?

Well, I will try to answer some of these questions now.

Ralph Coates – Bargain Buy

RALPH COATES cost Tottenham £190,000 when he moved from Burnley. People are still asking was he worth that much?

I'll always remember Coates for the chasing he gave Chelsea in the first half of a Cup replay at Burnley. That was our hardest Cup game of the season, tougher even than our two Finals against Leeds. And the reason for it was this great little player – Ralph Coates.

Can you spot the Ghost – Martin Peters

MARTIN PETERS is the ghost player of football because the fans scarcely notice him and rarely appreciate his skills. But top professionals on the park who plays against Peters can understand why Spurs paid £200,000 for him – and here's why.

McFarland's the best

Who is the best centre-half in Britain? Well, I've played against most of them and I'm convinced that Roy McFarland of Derby is not only the best centre-half in this country, he's the best in Europe, possibly the world.

King of the Heavy Mob

You have to be brave and strong to play as a striker in modern football, it also helps if you are big.

How to win without trying

Fifteen minutes to go and you are a goal ahead. Now the problem is – how to survive until the final whistle.

Football coaches have examined the situation, as with every other that can conceivably arise in the top-class game, and they have come up with their answer.

Shown here are some of the tricks used by professional players when they merely need to kill such time as the last few minutes of a Cup-tie.

The whole business may seem trivial but it is reckoned that with a few seconds lopped off here and there a total can be achieved that seems staggering.

In fact, it has been calculated that a team of experts can cut the last fifteen minutes of any match to around four minutes of actual play.

SO THE TEAM TRYING TO CATCH UP DOES NOT HAVE FIFTEEN MINUTES IN WHICH TO SCORE – ONLY FOUR.

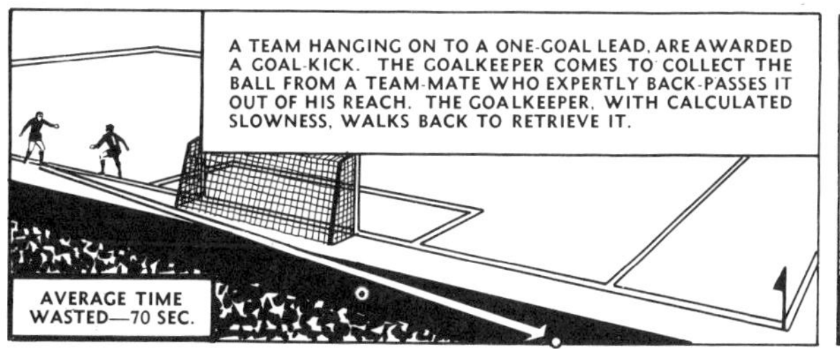

AVERAGE TIME WASTED—60 SEC.

IN A SIMILAR SITUATION, AN OPPONENT, DESPERATE TO SAVE TIME, CARRIES THE BALL BACK AND PLACES IT ON THE SIX-YARD LINE. THE GOALKEEPER RE-POSITIONS THE BALL ON A CAREFULLY SELECTED BUMP. AS HE MOVES BACK TO START HIS RUN-UP, THE BALL ROLLS OUT OF POSITION. THE GOALKEEPER CAN TAKE TWO, EVEN THREE, RUN-UPS BEFORE GETTING IT RIGHT.

A PLAYER AWARDED A FREE KICK PLACES THE BALL 10 YARDS AHEAD OF THE INCIDENT. "BACK," INSISTS THE REF, SO HE RETREATS FIVE YARDS—IT WON'T DO. BACK ANOTHER TWO YARDS, THEN TWO MORE. FINALLY, THE REF'S SATISFIED. UNNECESSARY OVERPLANNING OF THE KICK IS FOLLOWED BY A COMPLAINT THAT THE OPPOSITION ARE NOT 10 YARDS OFF THE BALL.

AVERAGE TIME WASTED—100 SEC.

WHEN THE BALL GOES INTO TOUCH, A PLAYER — KNOWING IT'S THE OTHER SIDE'S THROW— WILL QUICKLY TAKE IT. HE WILL FIND A TEAM-MATE WHO BOOTS IT ACROSS FIELD WHERE IT RUNS OUT OF PLAY. HE THEN PLAY-ACTS HIS ANNOYANCE AS THE REFEREE RECALLS THE THROW.

AVERAGE TIME WASTED—90 SEC.

AWARDED A THROW-IN, A PLAYER WILL SPEND AT LEAST 30 SECONDS PRETENDING TO TAKE IT BEFORE HANDING THE BALL TO A TEAM-MATE WHO THROWS IT STRAIGHT DOWN THE LINE, ENSURING IT NEVER ENTERS THE FIELD OF PLAY. HE HAS TO TAKE THE THROW AGAIN.

AVERAGE TIME WASTED—45 SEC.

A FORWARD WILL RUN TOWARDS A CORNER FLAG WHERE HE SHIELDS THE BALL UNTIL AN OPPONENT, IN DESPERATION, CONCEDES A CORNER.
UNDER THE PRETEXT OF TAKING A SHORT CORNER, HE CALLS IN A TEAM-MATE. A DEFENDER FOLLOWS, SO DOES A COMPLAINT—THE OPPOSITION ARE NOT 10 YARDS FROM THE BALL.

AVERAGE TIME WASTED—100 SEC.

No-One matches Moore

BOBBY MOORE or BILLY BREMNER? Given a straight choice whom would you pick? Bremner, who always plays at steam-heat or Moore, who looks as though he's chiselled out of an iceberg? It's a question that demands an answer – I hope my choice doesn't upset too many people in Leeds!

Royle – The Action-Man

DOUGAN and ROYLE are two upfield strikers, they tackle the toughest job in football. Here I have analysed their different styles, I've also picked the one I would prefer to have in my team.

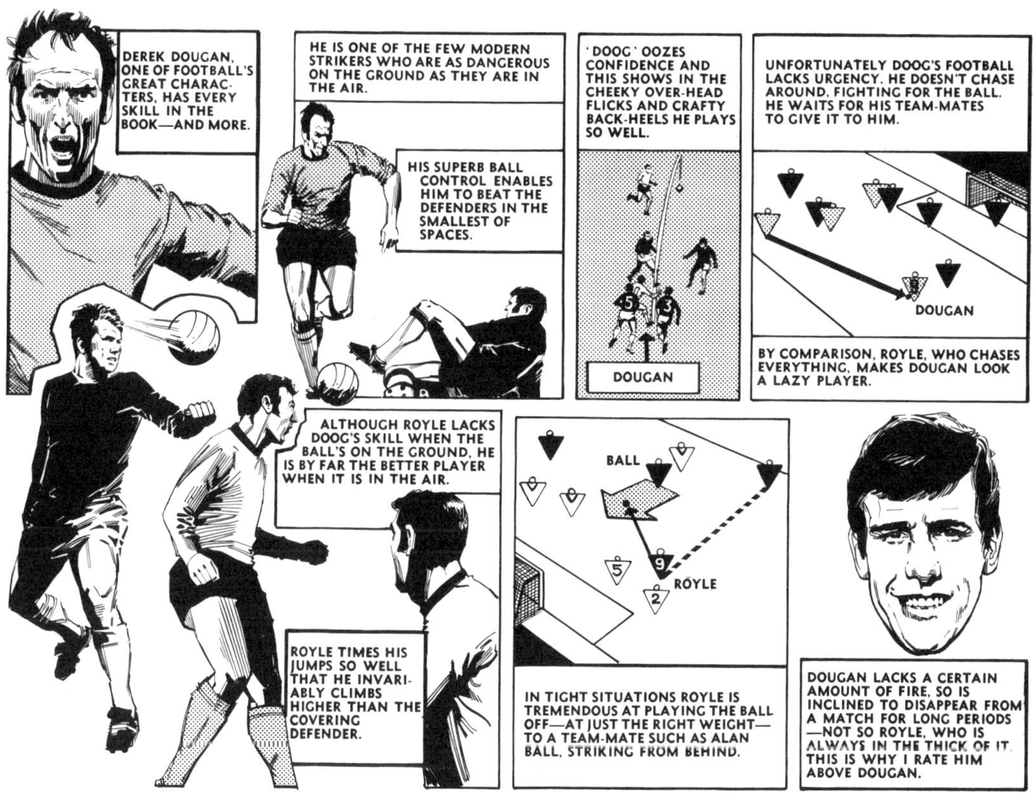

A Winning Double

JOHN HOLLINS and ALAN MULLERY are two human dynamos but who is the better player? Well, quite frankly I believe they are a winning double.

Hard-Man Hunter

NORMAN HUNTER, Leeds, and TOMMY SMITH, Liverpool are two of the tough guys of football. It's not much fun being tackled by either!

McNab Wins on Speed

BOB McNAB of Arsenal and CYRIL KNOWLES of Tottenham are two of the top defenders in this country. Both are excellent players – but one is a shade better and I will tell you why.

Look Out Super-Boy

TREVOR FRANCIS is one of football's greatest success stories. The fans chant 'Super – Super – Super-Boy' and it seems he can do no wrong. But here we look at the problems that are going to come his way soon.

How the other half live

Most players will tell you that the average fan only sees half of what really goes on in a football match. For instance – do you know why some players never seem to stop talking during a game?

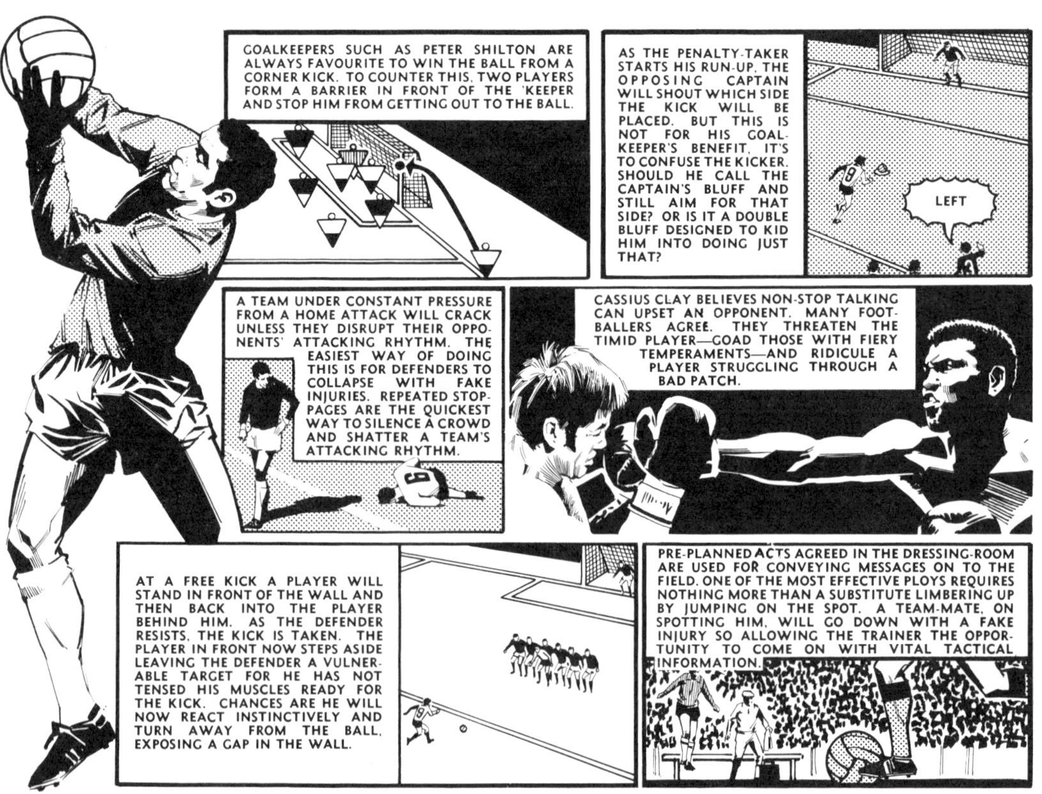

The Bomber

TONY BROWN of West Brom. misses very little, certainly nothing in the penalty area. He may not play for a fashionable team, but I still rate him above his opposite rival COLIN BELL of Manchester City.

Golden Goals

They may look golden goals, some of those spectacular scoring efforts, but a top footballer's opinion of a goal, as with so much else in the game, is usually very different from the view of the fan on the terrace or in front of a television screen.

Prince of Players

PELE is the greatest footballer the world has ever seen, and when Chelsea went up against him on one of our overseas tours, I had this proved to me over and over again.

Kick's don't intimidate me

Crunch – the tackle goes in, a player is carried off hurt and the cry goes up 'He asked for it, he wasn't wearing shin pads.'

But it's not that simple – I do not wear shin pads, and I never will.

ALAN HUDSON

BILLY BREMNER

STEVE PERRYMAN

MIKE CHANNON

DEREK DOUGAN

MARTIN CHIVERS

PETER SHILTON

DAVID WAGSTAFFE

TREVOR FRANCIS

ROY McFARLAND

FRANCIS LEE

BOBBY MOORE

MALCOLM MacDONALD

FRANK McLINTOCK

EMLYN HUGHES

COLIN TODD

JACKIE CHARLTON

JOHN RADFORD

GEORGE ARMSTRONG

TONY CURRIE

STEVE KEMBER

ASA HARTFORD

COLIN BELL

CHARLIE GEORGE

ALAN BALL

The Running Jump

No player can run backwards and jump his full height – a backward jump is always a falling jump.

An aerial artist such as PETER OSGOOD, Chelsea, will move AWAY from the player about to centre the ball.

Osgood has now created space into which he can run and so meet the ball at the top of his jump.

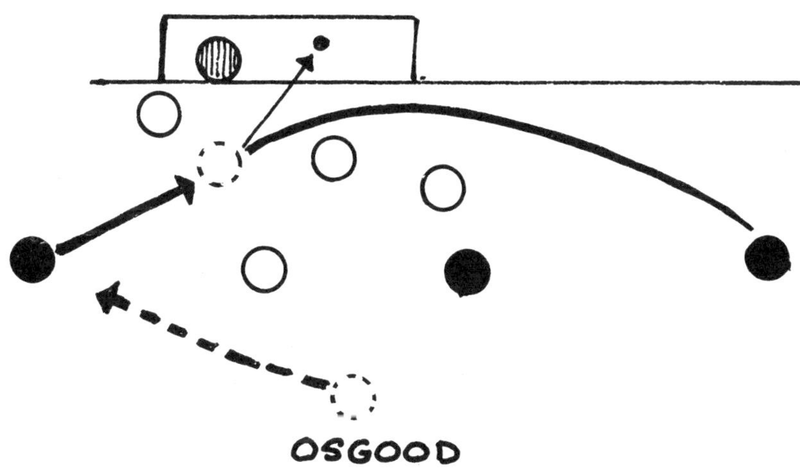

Reducing the shooting angle

When a forward is through on his own, PETER BONETTI, Chelsea, is very quick to move off his line and reduce the shooting angle.

In this type of situation Bonetti never over-runs.

The moment the shooting angle is covered, he stops – extra steps achieve nothing, they only increase the lobbing area above his head.

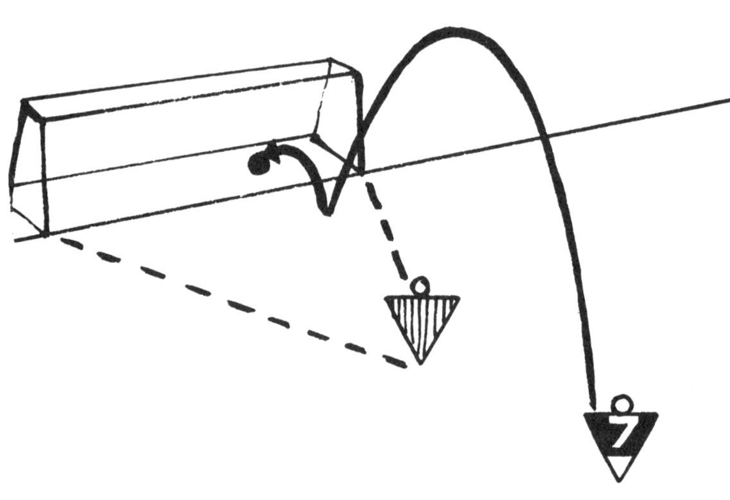

Decoy throw

The long throwing ability of Tottenham's MARTIN CHIVERS is often used as a decoy at throw-ins.

In the diagram, Chivers has run forward as if to take the throw. A team-mate already on the touchline prepares to hand the ball to Chivers. As the defending team drops back to guard against the long throw, Chivers's team-mate catches them out by throwing the ball into the free space created behind Chivers. A Spurs player, alert to this tactical pre-planned move, will dart forward, collect the ball and go for goal.

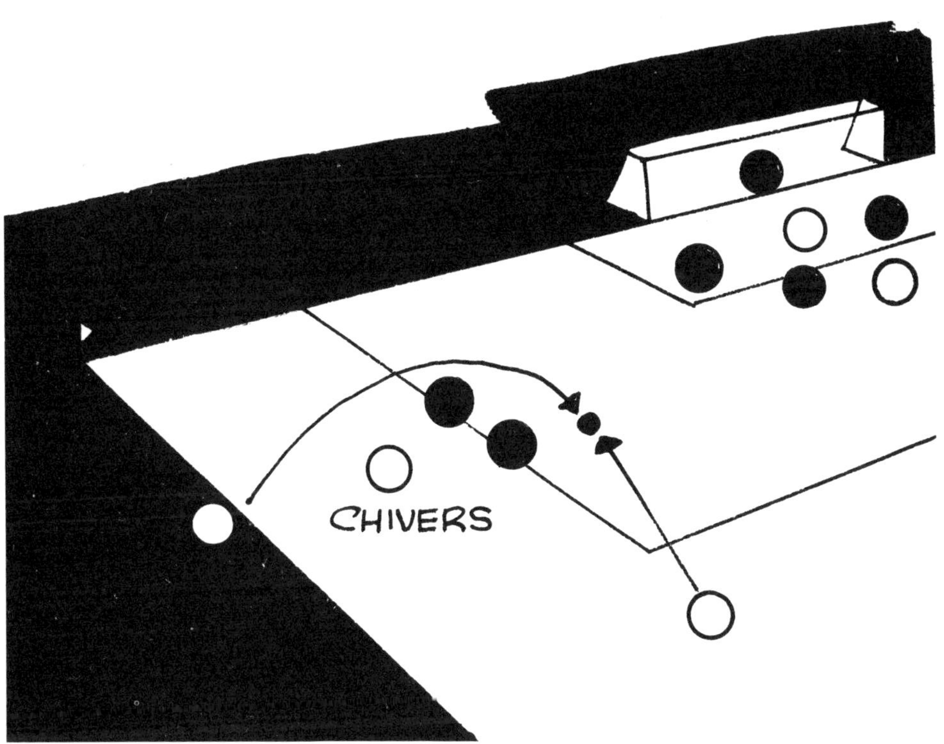

Space finder

In the diagram, IAN MOORE, Manchester United, has moved forward (taking a close-marking defender with him and so creating space at the back) to collect a pass.

Player 'A' in possession now hits the ball to Moore and races forward pointing ahead to where he wants a return pass.

But player 'A' will not receive the ball for his is only a decoy run devised to attract attention from player 'B' who moves forward to collect the ball Moore skilfully glances behind him.

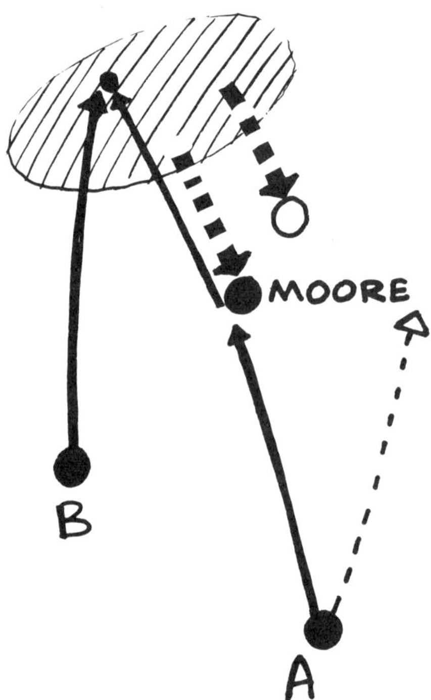

Straight run

When in possession STEVE HEIGHWAY of Liverpool will run directly at the full-back giving him no time to angle him into a negative position.

The defender is now left with one of two alternatives – retreat – and nobody can run as fast backwards as forwards – or move into a tackle and stand the risk of having the ball pushed past him with Heighway in pursuit.

Unless the defender has cover behind, the odds are Heighway will beat him every time.

Half-and-half

When top defenders like Arsenal's FRANK McLINTOCK find themselves faced by two forwards, they back-off slightly, keeping both players in sight and themselves in a half-and-half position ready to pounce on any forward pass.

By adopting these tactics, McLintock temporarily slows their progress so allowing time for his team-mates to fall back and cover.

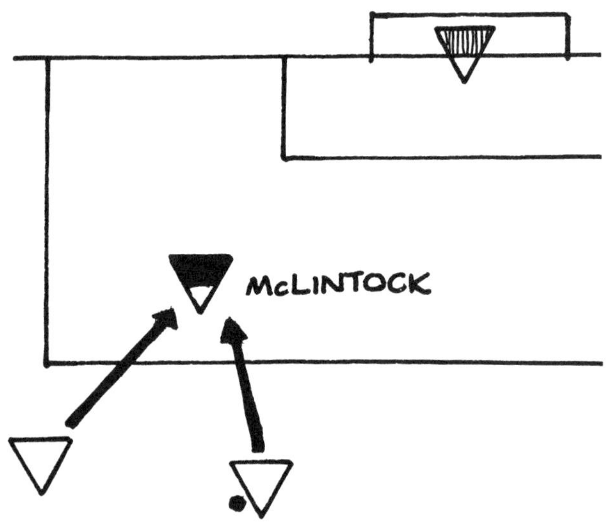

Keep mobile

An upfield striker must keep mobile – those who restrict their movements to inside the penalty box not only allow themselves to be tightly marked, they always have their backs to goal.

By varying his play, at times dropping back into his own half, EUSEBIO allows himself a greater area of the field in which to lose both his 'shadow' and express himself.

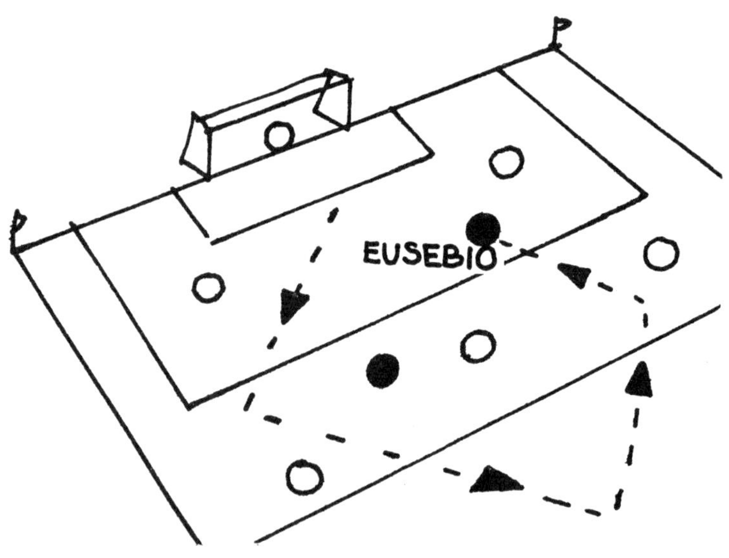

The Waiting Game

MALCOLM MACDONALD of Newcastle often appears in the penalty-box unmarked to finish off a goal move.

MacDonald's secret is a simple one – he delays his run so as not to alert the defenders in the box. Taking up a blind side position MacDonald waits until the ball is actually in flight and then, when the defenders have their eyes on the moving ball, he makes use of his explosive speed to race unnoticed onto the ball.

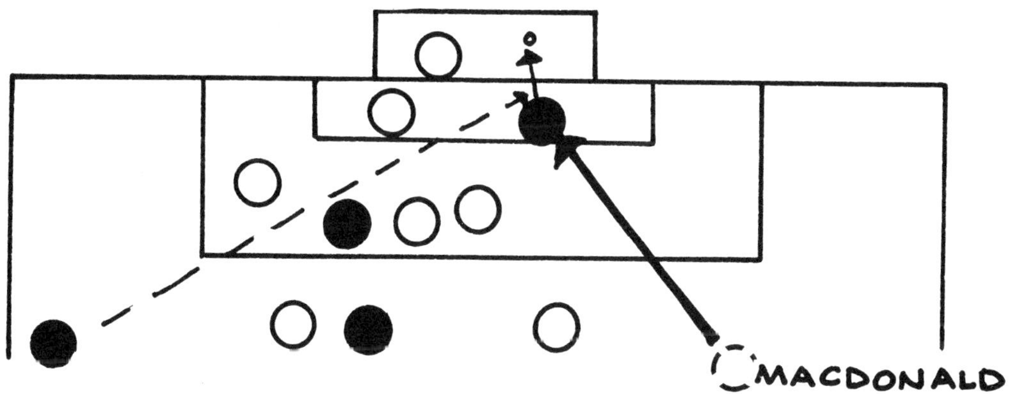

Cricket Clue

BOBBY MOORE rarely makes a careless pass – and here he lets us in on his secret.

'While the ball is still fifty yards away' says Bobby, 'a player should be summing up everyone's position, like a batsman storing up in his mind a picture of how all the opposing fieldsmen are placed. Then when the ball arrives the player can hit it at once to the exact spot.'

Furthermore, because you already know who is best placed to take the pass, you have that split second to disguise your action – possibly by a feint – so drawing opponents away and increasing the value of the pass.

Shielding the ball

The ban on tackles from behind has encouraged players to shield the ball more with their bodies.

CLYDE BEST of West Ham is a master at it. If an opponent attempts to tackle him on his left side, Best will immediately switch the ball to his right foot.

If the tackle threatens on his right side, he'll switch the ball to his left foot.

This means for the defender to rob Best of the ball he will have to stretch his leg across the front of Best's path, which is almost impossible to do by fair means.

Reverse turn

When MIKE SUMMERBEE, Manchester City, is tightly marked he will repeatedly move in the opposite direction to where he wants to go.

In the diagram, Summerbee has moved for a ball which his running indicates will be aimed to his left. The close-marking defender follows and then Summerbee suddenly changes direction.

This sudden reverse turn enables Summerbee to get in front of his marking defender and into a good position to receive the ball.

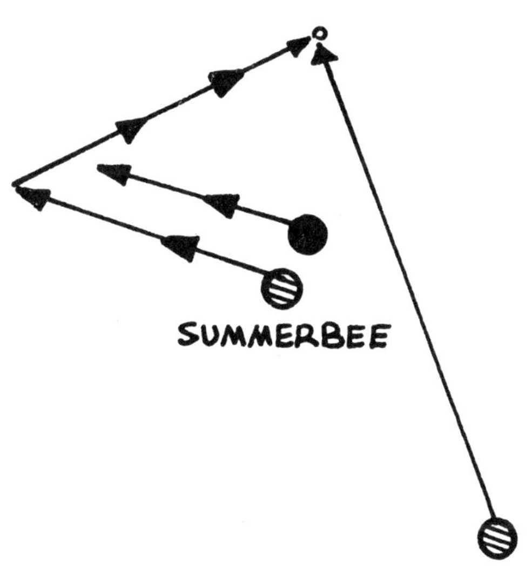

The Acting Game

Liverpool have often been known to put on a highly professional act when taking a throw-in.

Wing-half TOMMY SMITH and a team-mate will both take the ball for a Liverpool throw-in. They then give the impression of fighting over who will take the throw.

This is the cue for a Liverpool player to steal up into space. The ball is then quickly thrown to him while the opposition is still wondering which one will win the 'argument'.

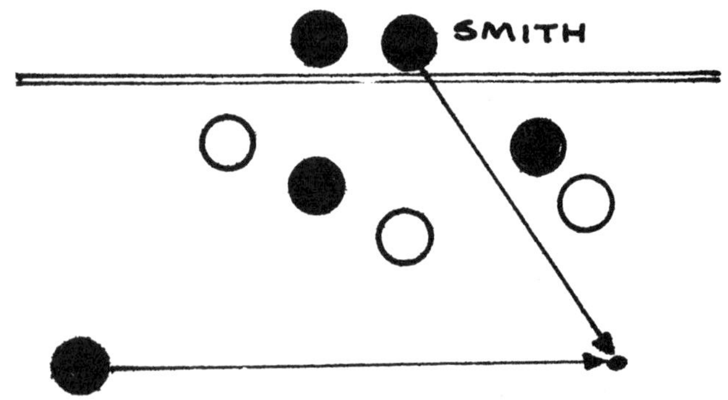

Controlling the tempo

When a team slows the game down, it has nothing to do with the speed in which it carries out its movements. It simply involves controlling the direction of play.

In the diagram, Arsenal's ALAN BALL has hit the first pass in a triangular passing movement which has but one object – it is meant to draw opponents forward or, at least, encourage them not to RETREAT.

An over-use of the forward pass only results in defenders retreating en block so filling the space, the attacking team hope to exploit.

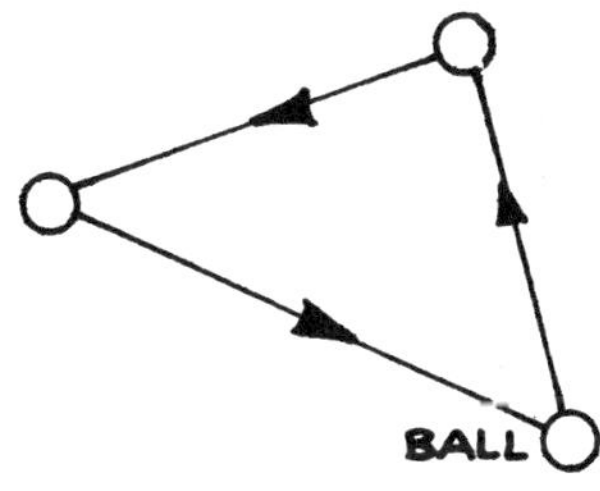

Animal cunning

Tottenham's MARTIN PETERS has never claimed to have an exceptional turn of speed – and yet he is always getting into advanced attacking positions where he can receive the ball and more often than not, finish with a goal effort.

Players who have a far greater turn of speed than Peters never get into these advanced attacking positions as effectively because they commit the sin of running TOO OBVIOUSLY and TOO OFTEN.

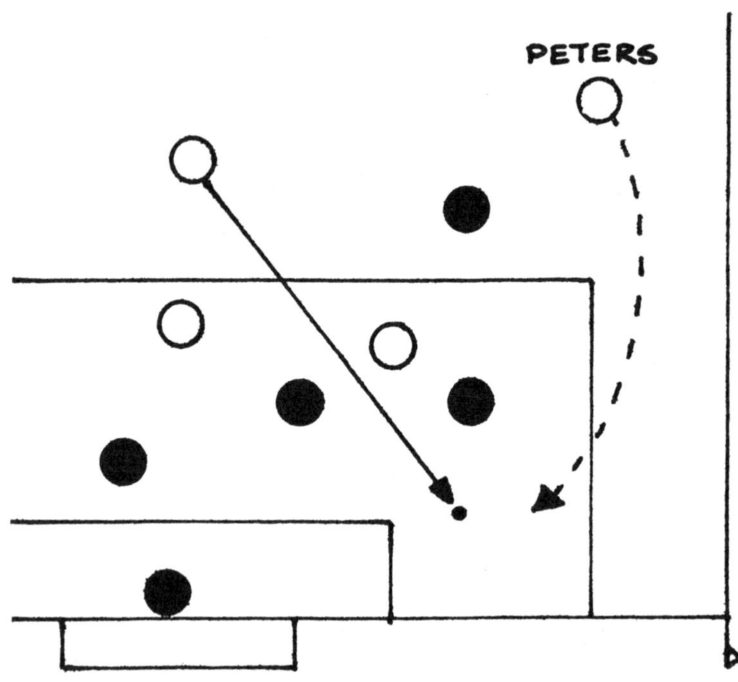

The Art of Concentration

'All players have momentary lapses of concentration' admits GORDON BANKS, Stoke.

'When I find my concentration wavering,' says Banks, 'I have a real go at myself.

'"KEEP YOUR MIND ON YOUR JOB, BANKS" I say, I slap my thighs – even pinch myself. I remember one game, we won 5–0 when I never touched the ball, and my thighs were black and blue with pinch marks.'

Tension Free

The beautifully balanced running of ALLAN CLARKE of Leeds, is possible because he is totally relaxed and loose of muscle.

Players who run with fists clenched and shoulders hunched bring tension into their strides and destroy their running rhythm.

One has only to look at the limp wrists and flapping hands of Clarke to detect he is free of muscle tension.

Pele, Best, Marsh and other good ball artists demonstrate this pianist technique.

Being First

'I usually consider the games in which I hardly make a tackle as being my best' says RON HARRIS, Chelsea.

'For this is the proof,' smiles Harris, 'that I was always first to the ball played up to my opponent. I also made the required interception when necessary and I kept so tight to my man, his team-mate usually considered it too big a risk to pass to him.'

Show Yourself

The golden rule when supporting a player on the ball is to run into a position where he can see you out of the corner of his eye.

It takes a special brand of cunning to be able to HIDE from defenders and yet still SHOW yourself to your team-mates.

A good example of this art of deception is PELE, who breaks quickly on the blind side of defenders facing the ball – yet at all times keeps himself within view of his team-mate on the ball.

Stabbing Action

There are times when Tottenham's MARTIN CHIVERS in a ruck of players, hasn't the room for a full swing so he stabs the ball home.

This STABBING ACTION – where the ball is kicked close to the non-kicking foot – enables the forward simply to turn his foot an inch or so either way to completely alter the direction of the shot. This means the opposing goalkeeper is denied the opportunity of anticipating the direction the ball will travel.

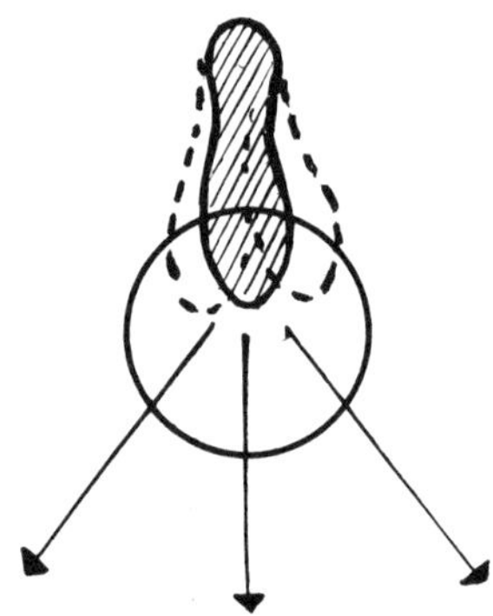

Keep Mobile

For a forward, goal to goal running is not always a good thing. For instance, in the diagram, if the three upfield strikers waiting on a through-pass all go for goal, so will the defenders leaving the player in possession no space to exploit up front.

Mobile forwards like KEVIN KEEGAN of Liverpool, move in all directions – either back, forward or to the wing – in order to pull the opposing defenders out of position so creating space into which a forward pass can be played.

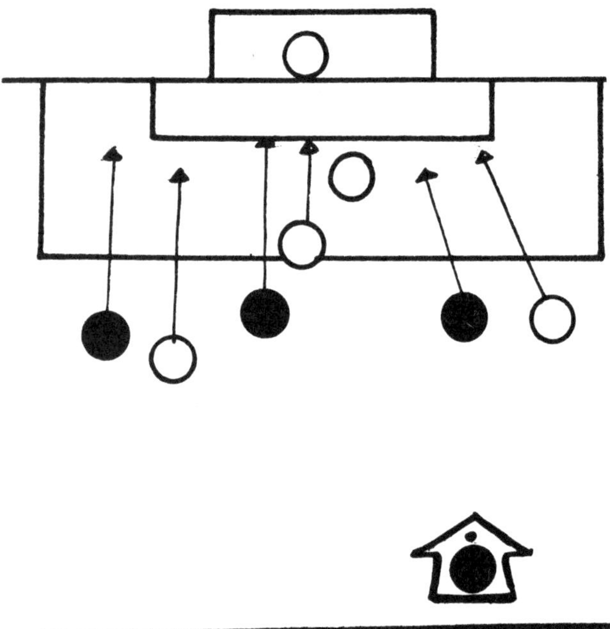

Smart Thinking

With the awarding of a free-kick, the penalized side form a wall to cover half of the goal, the remaining goal space to be guarded by the goalkeeper.

Smart-thinking goalkeepers such as GORDON BANKS, Stoke, will occasionally deliberately position themselves more to one side so leaving the kicker an unguarded area of goal to aim at. Only in that vital last second, as the kicker makes contact, will the goalkeeper correct the situation by moving across to make what will now be a comparatively simple save.

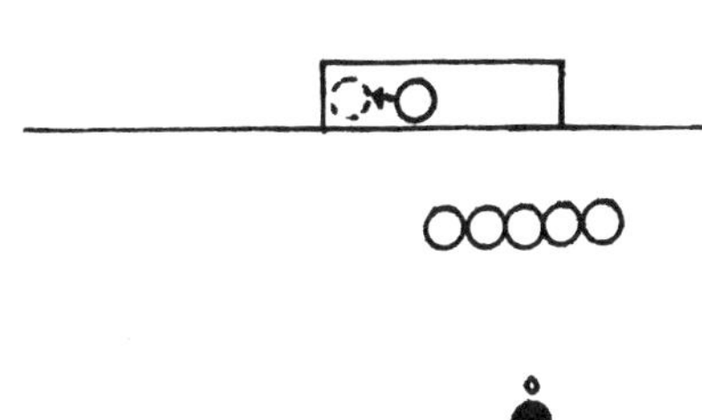

Negative Play

Top managers like BILL SHANKLY of Liverpool will be the first to tell you that deliberate offside play is the most negative act in football.

Agreed, the defending side is awarded a free kick, but because its own forwards are so closely marked before the kick is taken – excepting territory – no advantage is gained.

A team operating the offside trap as a means of defence simply denies itself the opportunity of launching a quick counter attack, and so possibly catching the opposition stretched at the back.

Forward March

Watch how Leicester's goalkeeper PETER SHILTON moves well out from his goal when the opposition are under heavy fire.

This serves two purposes – not only is Shilton perfectly positioned to deal with the long through ball designed to set up a counter attack, he is also out of earshot of spectators behind his goal whose remarks could easily upset his concentration.

Ignoring the Ball

Top defenders like NOBBY STILES are quick to read a 'wall pass' and act accordingly.

When the player on the ball attempts a 'wall pass' with a colleague, Nobby will not watch the initial pass – instead he will turn quickly and race to collect the return ball ahead of the forward.

Feinting

Watch the way top players like CHARLIE GEORGE will feint to hit a pass one way and in many cases it's not until the ball is actually in flight, that one realises it is going in another direction.

Because defenders mark space as tightly as they mark players, feinting is as important in passing as it is in dribbling.

If a defender can be hoodwinked into misreading a situation he can be lured away from the point of attack so leaving space for exploitation.

Direction Plus Distance

The two main ingredients of every good pass are:

1. DIRECTION – the target area to be hit.

2. DISTANCE – the ground to be covered.

There's no problem in aiming the ball at the target, but only exceptional players like PELE see things 'bird's-eye' view and can apply the correct pace to passes ranging from four to forty feet.

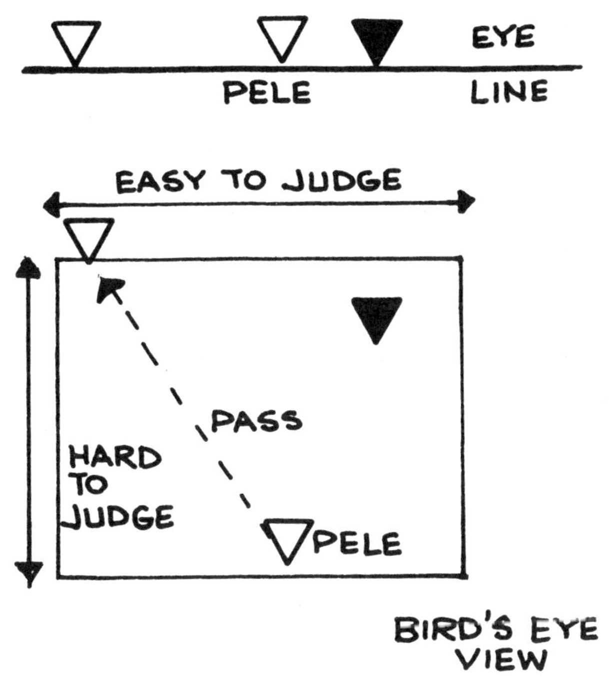

Telepathy

A forward such as TOMMY HUTCHISON, Blackpool, does not have to have eyes in the back of his head to know there is a team-mate positioned behind him who is in a better scoring position.

In the diagram the wing man (A) has skilfully flighted the ball well short of the near post. Forward (B) has to run out to what was a tight scoring position to get to the ball. This tells (B) he is meant to back-head the ball to a colleague better placed waiting behind.

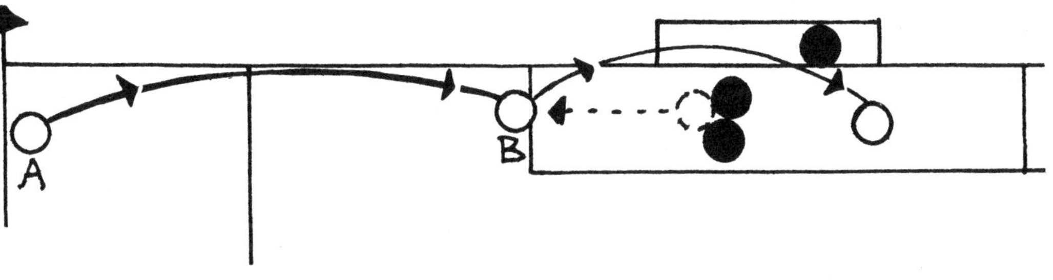

Cover the Ball

When FRANCIS LEE of Manchester City goes for goal he keeps his weight well forward with his upper torso covering the ball. This body forward position enables Lee to hit the ball both hard and low without first checking his speed.

In a similar situation, less gifted players have to check slightly in order to position themselves correctly and it is this hesitation which allows a defender to get in a tackle.

Space Age

The vital decision of when to mark tight and when to cover is the most important one a defender has to make. The back four must ensure space is never created *behind* them into which the ball can be played for an attacker to run onto.

In the diagram, Tottenham's STEVE PERRYMAN has ignored the man nearest him and has raced back to mark the space which, for a split-second, was there for the attacking team to exploit.

PERRYMAN

'Touch' Player

A 'touch' player like JON SAMMELS of Leicester is highly skilled at hiding five to ten yards in a pass without any alteration to his kicking action.

In the diagram it appears SAMMELS has passed to 'A' and 'A' keeps up the pretence by moving towards the ball and in doing so pulls the defender out of position.

'B' alert to the situation races behind 'A' to collect the ball which runs on due to the concealed extra pace.

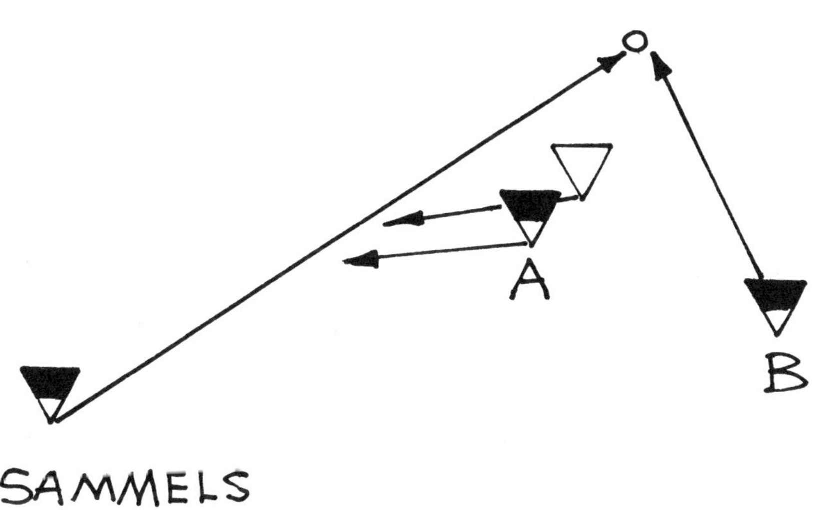

Angles and Angles

When JOHNNY GILES of Leeds, is in possession he is always moving to make a better angle to deliver a pass. Likewise the forwards up front are moving to make better angles to receive the ball.

In the diagram (A) has intelligently run to the left before reversing to collect a through ball. If he had not moved, defender (B) would have been favourite to cut off the pass.

Outside is Best Side

Top ball players such as DENIS LAW, Manchester United, learn to control the ball with the *outside* of their foot.

The ball controlled with the inside of the foot is directed *towards* the defender; the ball controlled with the outside of the foot is directed *away* from him.

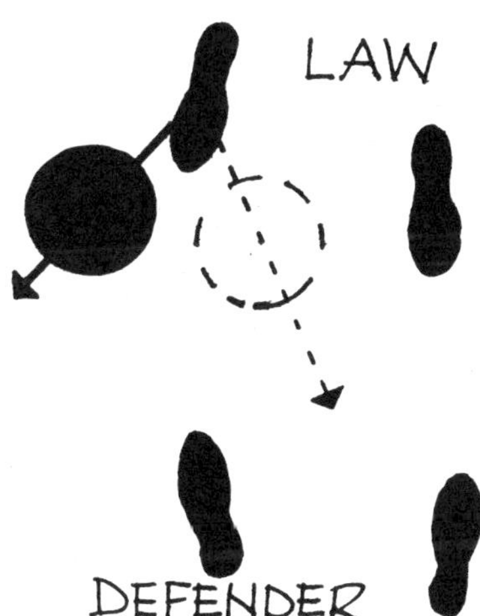

Target Area

When a centre's on, upfield strikers like JOHN TOSHACK, Liverpool, ensure they have space between themselves and the other forward runner. This way Toshack simplifies the problem for the player centering the ball. Instead of having to hit a target area of, say, six feet, he can now float the ball into space for the forward in the most favourable position to run on and meet.

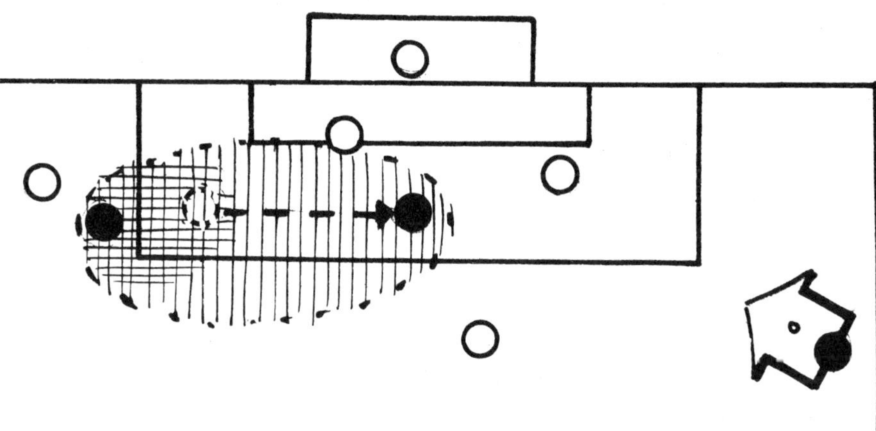

Stranded

Expert corner-kickers like TERRY PAINE of Southampton will flight successive kicks to the edge of the six-yard box, forcing the goalkeeper to leave his line in an effort to deal with them.

The trap set, the kick will be hit with the inside of the foot producing an outswinger which lures the goalkeeper out of his goal – only this time to be left stranded.

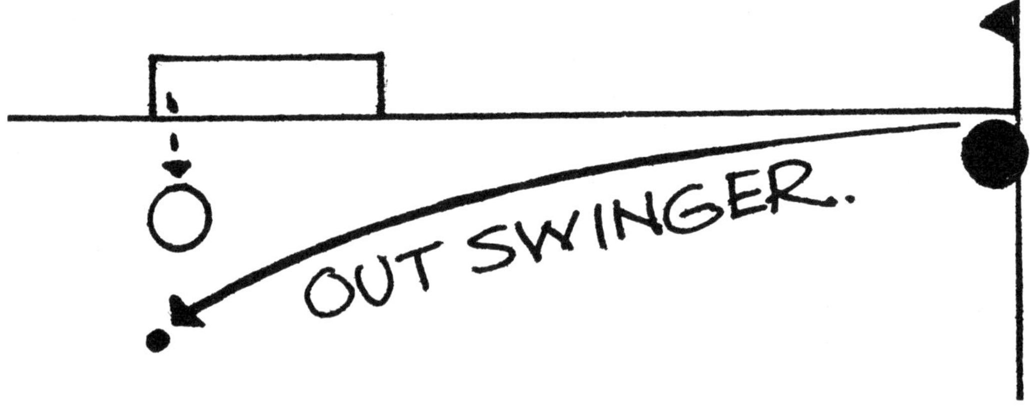

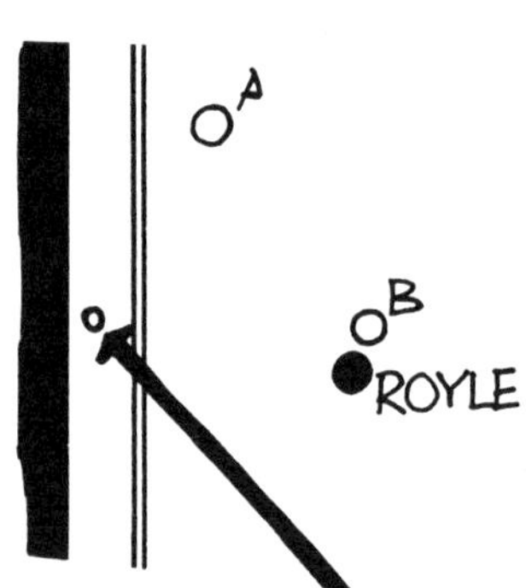

Fools Rush In

There are times when hard running forwards such as JOE ROYLE, Everton, will not chase a ball obviously going out of play for a throw-in – and there is always a good reason for this as the diagram illustrates.

Should Royle lose his race for the ball, defender A can take a quick throw-in to his unmarked team-mate B, so getting a quick counter-attack started.

Royle offsets this by staying put so marking B out of the throw.

Be Positive

Confidence in goal communicates confidence to the whole team. No goalkeeper demonstrates this better than Manchester United's goalkeeper, ALEX STEPNEY. The goalkeeper who is always changing his mind – one moment going for the ball, the next retreating to his line – throws confusion into every defender.

A goalkeeper should be positive in everything he does. When he goes out for a high cross he must be prepared to knock even his own players out of the way in his determination to be first to the ball.

Support Your Team-Mates

When a top defender such as JACKIE CHARLTON, Leeds, gains possession in a crowded goalmouth, he knows he must part with the ball as quickly as possible – for every additional second that he holds onto it his chances of being caught in possession are increased. Charlton's colleagues up front must now support him by running into good positions.

In the diagram (A) has run behind defender (B), his team-mate (C) immediately runs forward to be in a position to receive a pass. If the covering defender stays with forward (A), (C) will receive the ball. Alternatively if defender (B) follows forward (C) the ball will be chipped over their heads to forward (A).

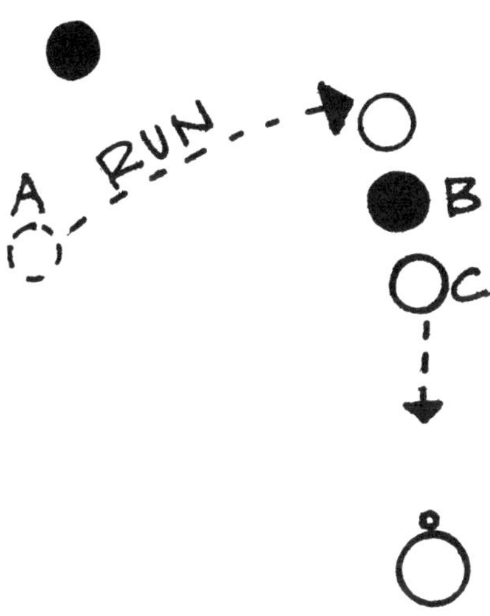

Pass-Back and Attack

When BOBBY MOORE calls to a hard-pressed defender for a pass-back it is, in most cases, an attacking movement.

Moore, who plays behind the back four, is in a position to see all his colleagues and has more time to select where to make a penetrating pass, whereas the hard-pressed defender, in most cases, is facing the wrong way.

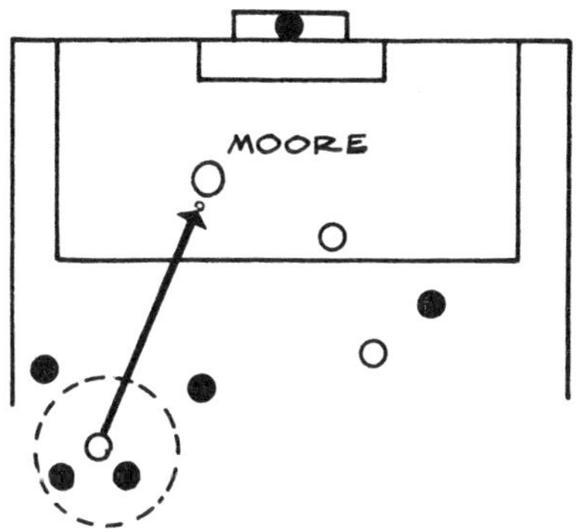

Selling a Dummy

Top strikers like RON DAVIES of Southampton will feint to go one way (taking a defender with them) before racing to the area in front of goal laid down in tactic talks as the real target zone.

In the diagram, Davies, realizing a centre is on, starts a decoy run to the far post. The dummy sold, Davies then changes direction losing the close-marking defender and so making space for himself to meet the ball directed towards the near post.

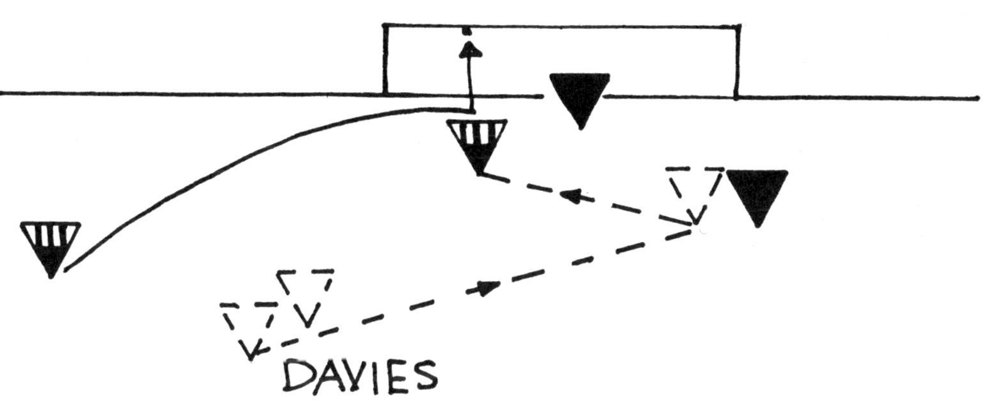

Wind Brake

Top soccer brains like Manchester City's MALCOLM ALLISON will be quick to tell you that a crosswind does not necessarily spoil a game, providing the teams use it to their advantage.

For example, when attacking, play into the wind – then passes hit hard to avoid interception are wind-braked and do not overrun team-mates.

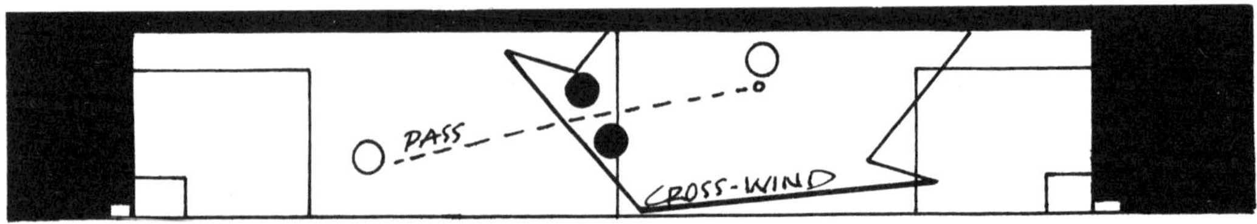

Penalty-Spot Guide

Master of the shooting angles is England and Stoke goalkeeper GORDON BANKS. He knows the moment the ball leaves the forward's foot whether it is on target or not.

The penalty-spot can prove an accurate guide for determining the direction of shots hit outside the penalty box.

Any shot passing wide of that mark (except for a very small area in front of goal) will pass wide of the posts.

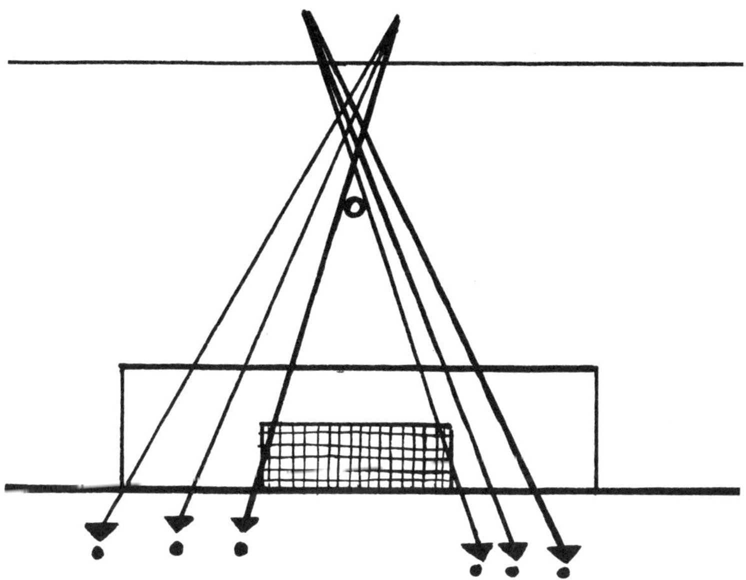

Long Throw

Arsenal's JOHN RADFORD's long throw presents more danger to a defence than a corner kick.

This is because the ball comes in at a different trajectory and HANGS at the end of its flight. Defenders and forwards join forces UNDER the ball and it is in this build-up of bodies that tall players dominate.

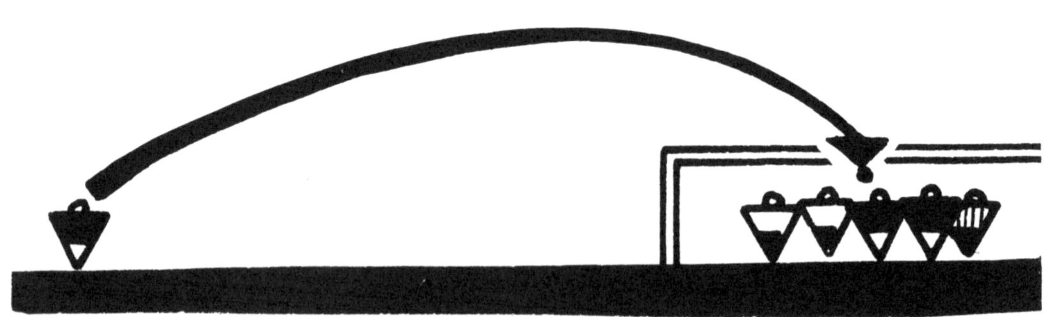

Freezes Out

JIMMY JOHNSTONE of Celtic, who requires double-marking, often sets up goal chances without touching the ball.

By moving to pre-planned positions, Johnstone pulls the key defenders out of position and then freezes them to the spot while his team-mates exploit the gaps their absence has created.

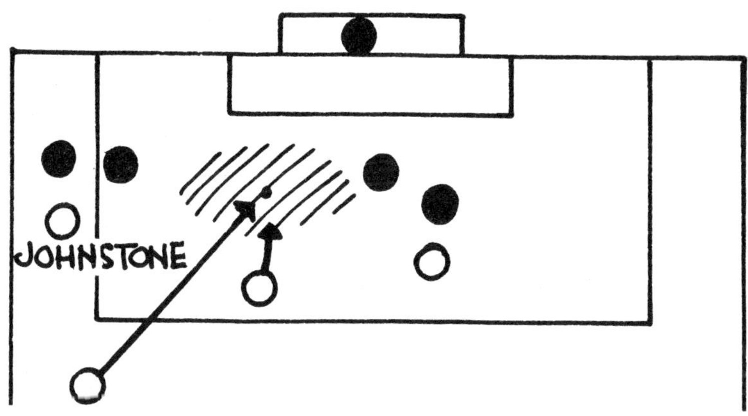

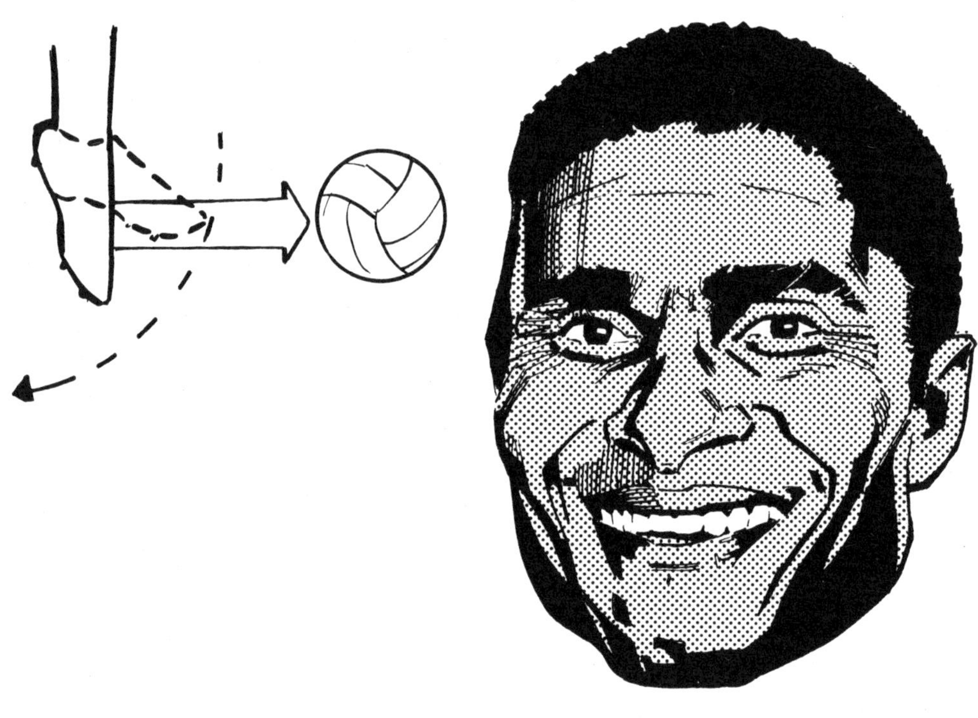

Dropped Ankle Technique

'How did he miss that?' is what the terrace fans say when a forward, completely unmarked and standing practically underneath the bar, blazes the ball over.

In most cases the forward, surprised by his good fortune, swings too quickly – snatches at the ball – catching it high on an instep already pointing skywards. In a similar situation EUSEBIO adopts the DROPPED ankle technique where the toe drops to point to the ground enabling a flat hitting surface to be presented to the ball.

Team Tactics

Team-work is the basis of all great sides, and this is why even great individual players like GEORGE BEST have to conform within a tactical framework of a side.

But this doesn't mean that Best is shackled by the system. If and when he finds himself in a position where he can go it alone, he will.

Great players like Best have the DISCIPLINE to conform to team tactics, and more important – the IMAGINATION to go for the unexpected.

Skill on the Ball

The most common criticism levelled at PELE is that he shies away from tough tackling.

This is nonsense! It's thanks to his skill on the ball that he can EVADE a tackle rather than take one.

Diagonal Pass

ROY McFARLAND of Derby is a fabulous passer of a ball.

Nobody hits a diagonal pass with more accuracy. McFarland will place it near enough to a defender to tempt him forward and yet far enough away to elude him so cutting him out of the game.

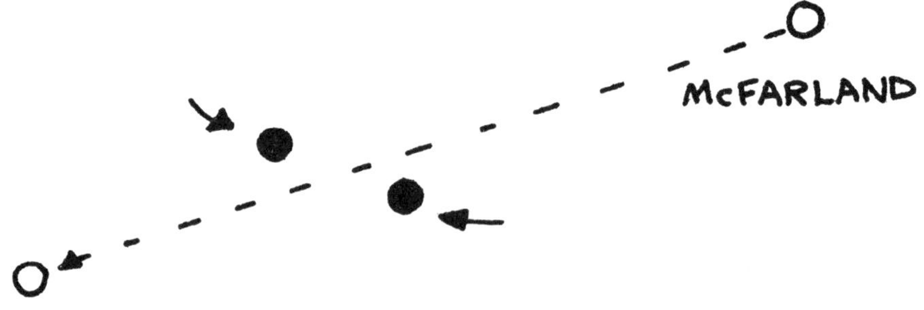

Two Minds

When a forward breaks through on his own, GORDON BANKS is very quick to leave his line. By coming out quickly, Banks puts the forward in two minds – whether to shoot or dribble round him. This slight hesitation on the forward's part could give the keeper the time to dive at his feet or allow a defender to drop back and cover.

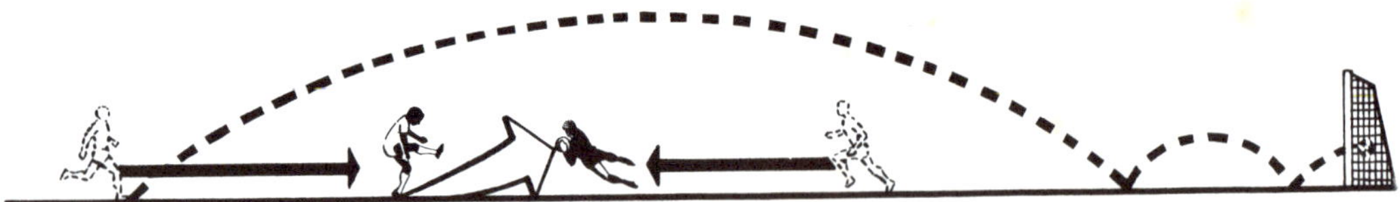